UNEQUAL THIRDS

Annie

All the very best.

Tim

UNEQUAL THIRDS

Tim Cunningham

PETERLOO POETS

First published in 2006
by Peterloo Poets
The Old Chapel, Sand Lane, Calstock,
Cornwall PL18 9QX, U.K.

A catalogue record for this book is available
from the British Library

ISBN 1-904324-34-7

Printed by 4word Ltd,
Unit 15, Baker's Park, Cater Road, Bristol BS13 7TT

ACKNOWLEDGEMENTS

To date, some of these poems have appeared in, or been accepted for publication by:

Acumen
The Betjemanian
The Burning Bush
Candelabrum
Chimera
Cyphers
Dreamcatcher
Envoi
Exile
The Frogmore Papers
The Interpreter's House
Khimera
Krax
The Limerick Leader
Littoral
Magma
Microphone On
Nomad
Peterloo Poetry Competition Anthology
Poetry Ireland
Seam
The Shop
Smiths Knoll
Sol
Stony Thursday
Wasafiri

Supported by
The National Lottery®
through Arts Council England

For Norma

CONTENTS

Mouse

Time scratches the floorboards,
Scurries, soft and furry,
On pink feet. I plugged
The mouseholes like some rodent dyke,
Flattening polish tins
And nailing lids down
With the guilt of crucifixion.
Such unheroic shields.
Every night, the baiting of traps
With bread, with nuggets of cheese.
Each morning, a plopped
Disposal in the yard,
Except the tiny one I freed,
The baby caught by its terrified tail
And dragging the trap
Like a toy town horse and cart.

No droppings now on the breakfast table.
The house has shed
Its tenement skin, metamorphosed
To studios, surgeries,
The smart dot com address.
The only holes are power points.
The only mouse sends arrows
Scurrying round the VDU
Or sleeps by its computer:
Hairless, no appetite for cheese,
Its long tail tapering
To the back of the machine.
The click at the touch of a finger
Has nothing on the snap of a midnight
Trap. And never a panic
In its plastic breast.

The Face in the Mirror

The face in the mirror was not mine.
Standing, sleeves rolled up, by the fire,

Washing her hands in a basin
Propped on the old tea-chest, drying

Them on a red and white tea-
Towel, her image was clear as day.

Turning confirmed that nobody
Was there; the enamel basin empty.

Talk of hallucinations, the mechanics
Of the eye, the cliché trick

Of the light have never convinced.
A premonition of absence

Comes closer to felt truth,
And I imagine clues

Might lie in where she was just then
And what exactly she was doing:

Tomb-tight secrets. More
And more, I wonder where

She is and what she might
Be doing. And when she ignites

Memory, it is the face in the mirror
That I clearly see

And the tea-towel, like a chequered
Flag, reminding me her race is over.

'Gone with the Wind'

The night before he went to war,
He bought her favourite chocolates
And they sat snug in the balcony seats
Of the old Savoy.

Their love burned ardent as Atlanta.
He never said he didn't give a damn,
And she didn't say,
'Tomorrow is another day.'

Confusing promise and wish,
His last words echoed, 'I'll be back.'
Those beautiful, fragile, butterfly words
Fluttering in the breeze.

She kept the chocolate box as souvenir.
It's where she kept his letters:
The long ones written in blue ink,
The pencilled pages that he asked her

To rewrite in pen,
His words in the strange handwriting
Of the chaplain and an Irish nurse.
And then the telegram.

Toy Soldiers

After the war was over,
After he never came home
And her ears rang with the tinnitus
Of 'I'll be back' of 'I'll be back',

I laid siege to the vacuum,
Conscripted an army of words,
Dressed them in full battle
Gear with orders to smile,

To be versatile, to go over
The top with their tiny
Lead bayonets and do
The job on loneliness,

To stand guard round
The tea-time table, to sing
About how far to Tipperary,
To win back her no-man's-land.

It became a habit.
When I left the house
They followed me, singing
The essence of cobbled streets

And overcast skies,
Bearing the standard in every
Campaign, marching in step
Alert to the brass bugle's blast.

When she died, they formed
A guard of honour but refused
To retire. Asked why they still
Polish boots and buttons
And shuffle in battle fatigues,

They click their heels,
Stand to attention in stanzas
Or sometimes stand at ease.

But always the same explanation:
After the war was over,
After the flags were furled,
A young mother's husband

Didn't make it home.
Toy soldier words
Know the drill, ghosting
The limbo of 'I'll be back'.

Edge

He mellowed like autumn,
Lost his abrasive edge,
Assumed the wisdom
Of tired bodies, the orchard
Colours of drawn skin.

Freshly loved
For his tally of years, the slight
Droop of shoulder,
The endearing weakness of the mighty
Bowed if not broken, forgiven

The forgotten anger,
The flashing thrust and parry
Of his rapier tongue,
He was sanctified by time,
Cherished like nostalgic songs.

But I miss most
His bellow, his wholesome anger,
The thunder clap
Of fists against the table laying
Down the law like tablets of stone.

Tannery

Death by drowning was not in the stars
So they hauled him like a seal
From the tannery vat, wiped his face,
Towelled salts and acids from his leathering

Arms, watched the familiar swing
Of leg over saddle for the short ride home,
Uneasy as a picador with broken lance.
And the smell of death clung,

Squelched with his trousers, slipped
With his shoes at each push on the pedals.
The car sniffed it, snorted,
Charged like a bull through capes of mist.

Bayard

A quiet street of quiet lives:
Roses or chrysants in curtained windows,
Sparrows hopping on corrugated roofs,
Children dropping skipping ropes
To gaze up at the undertaker's horse,
The sleek black stallion
Outside my uncle's door
Waiting between funerals,
Harnessed to the mourners' black carriage,
Striking sparks with his impatient hoof.

The street is quieter now.
The skeleton has passed this way
Not with hour-glass and scythe
But driving his bulldozer,
Swinging his wrecking ball.

The flowers' flames are quenched.
The children's wings have long since
Spread above migrating winds.
What is left is the echo
Of a horse's iron shoe,
The sparks igniting memory.

Wheelwright

He rented the cobbled yard's workshop:
A young Thor hammering curved falloes,
Marrying them with planed ash spokes,
Wrenching the wheelband in white coals,
Dousing, beating it to a halo fit.

Rooted in dockleaves and dandelions,
They stood upright against the wall.
But painted wheels turned;
Gathering speed, spun backwards
Bemusing innocent eyes.

Doubt's first droplets sizzled on flame.
Soon the rattle of chariots scything
Through credos and catechism certainties,
And everywhere the snap and crunch of bones:
Beliefs, like martyrs, broken on a wheel.

Dirty Linen

The convent wall is broken,
The Magdalene laundry breached.
Too late for those who left
By the funeral door,

For lives too long sacrificed
At the steam-press's altar,
Folded and ironed beyond change.
Dropped at the convent

Like dirty linen parcelled
In brown paper and tied with string,
Some were soiled
With an instinct for life;

Some cried their stain in nightmares
Of a father's Judas kiss;
All bore the mark of 'Doesn't fit',
The unoriginal sin.

Even the nuns who were angels
Were angels with flaming swords,
Guarding gates to the everyday paradise;
Nuns whose mediaeval sisters

Were also walled away,
Knowing the hymen hymn
And the nipple's purple halo
Pulse with love.

Here, hymns to the Virgin Mother
Were music while they worked.
Undressing in bed,
Their nightdress shrouds

Extinguished luminous skin.
The permitted pulse beat
On Saturday nights,
The needle surfing records

Of a ceilidh band.
Women, hurting for the touch
Of children, family and lovers,
Danced together, each

To the rhythm of her own emptiness.
If Christ had stepped among them,
They would have washed His feet with tears.
In a world of our own,

We chalked goalposts
On their gable end;
Saw steam rise,
Without a thought of incense

Or the soft soot fallen over Europe.
Serving mass
In convent-tailored
Surplice and soutane,

I poured water
From a cut-glass cruet
Over the celebrant's fingers.
Drying them in the laundered fingertowel

With the little red two-stitch cross,
He prayed:
'I will wash my hands
Among the innocent.'

Eating Tim O'Brien

Inside the church, the barque of Peter,
They knelt in prayer for a fair wind
To swell their sails for the shore of heaven.
The gospel spoke of casting lots
For a seamless robe, and the congregation
Queued for Christ's unleavened body.
Candles took the chill from the pieta.

Another mother knelt outside
On stone sharp as Golgotha,
Hair wild as a winter blackthorn,
Outstretched arms forever empty,
Her supplication the curse of God
On Captain Gorman who passed her
On his way to Sunday mass.

The paperboys were raucous as the gulls,
Their foghorn voices shouting headlines
From *The Limerick Star*:
'*The Francis Spaight* becalmed',
'Lot Falls on Cabin Boy',
'Sea Captain Acquitted
By an English Court'.

'Garryowen Market, Limerick'

Turner's 'Garryowen' may not exist:
A conjecture of greens, blues
And browns subdued by Limerick mist.

Mine does, its lines pencilled
Indelibly with the matter-of-fact
Vision of a child's eye – until

Songs and history lessons coloured
And gave resonance to truth.
Then St. John's cathedral bell echoed

Sarsfield's armour on the anvil.
A stray piebald outside the school
Was Galloping Hogan's. The Model

T's backfire was Ballyneety's
Munition train exploding
Still across hurt centuries.

Apples whispered less of Eden
Than of Williamites' roasting taunts,
And women's role muscled from Virgin

Marys to defenders of the walls.
Their courage is celebrated
On the Treaty Stone's rough altar:

Our touchstone on the past, now
Sliding from St. Munchin's Church down
Clancy Strand; a black ice-floe

Dislodged by time, eroding clarity
The way a watercolour fades
Displayed in summer light.

The Treaty Stone

At the corner of history, the Treaty Stone
Stands, scans, from its limestone pedestal,
The muscular Shannon shouldering ships
And swans' reflections, supervises time and rain
Scrub the blood from King John's Castle and Thomond
Bridge. What matter if Ginkel and Sarsfield

Never signed a treaty on this stone, if its claim
To fame was to squat outside 'The Black Bull' inn
And help some farmer's wife mount pillion?
Nobody's philosopher's stone, no Moses tablet
Chiselled with commands. But for some
In that 'ancient city' like heroic Carthage 'schooled

In the hardships of war' an easy step to Pegasus,
A mass rock resonant with faith and fear,
A reliquary for shards of love, the faded baize
On which we threw the dice. For most, the muffled
Drum, the theatre that sutured unseen wounds,
The anvil chiming out the dream, the touchstone

Teaching fingers touch like Moore massaging
His mother's back or Hepworth in her father's car
Surfing the contours of the Yorkshire dales.
For all, the rock of the age of childhood
To which we pilgrim renewing the ancient pact,
And no two pens dipped in the same ink.

Siege

I love that city as if hair
Fell soft about its shoulders,
As if its eyes were lakes of naked joy
And its voice the music of spring.

I was no William outside its walls.
My feet caressed the pavement
Like a midnight skin as I searched
For the breach where love could penetrate.
I told the stones about my love
And the tongue in the stone was silent.

I loved the heat-hazed summers forging
Blood hot as the shoe
For Sarsfield's horse. He held the wall.
I held my heart like a roasted apple.
I told the fire about my love
And the tongue in the fire was silent.

I loved the streams where the salmon
Of knowledge swam, and Shannon's
Rippling shoulders that bore
French ships a treaty late.
I told the river about my love
And the tongue in the river was silent.

I loved the wind flapped
Down through history by wild geese
Wings, and the breeze that rushed
Round corners as if late for mass.
I told the wind about my love
And the tongue in the wind was silent.

And someone in that city had hair
That fell soft about her shoulders,
Eyes that were lakes of naked joy
And a voice the music of spring.

Token

Like whitewater rapids,
Dopamine rushes through veins,
Carves, in the gulleys and canyons
Of his brain, an ecstasy
As fervent as Bernini's marble saint.
And spring-tide oxytocin
Promises this flood will never
Ebb. Buoyed on hope,

He nests his dreams in the palm
Of her hand with his lucky stone
Smooth as skin, scrubbed
And polished by waves and wind,
Flat as his Swiss watch,
Light as a Vegas chip:
A small, if blemished sacrifice
Offered on a bloodless altar.

He wonders what relics the stone
Might hold: a pterodactyl
Wingbeat, the whiff of fear
At a phalanx of advancing ice,
The panic of an extinct gill,
A fleck of the great elk's
Antler locking horns
On some misty peak?

And all, perhaps, familiar
With the same surge
Chiselling the brain,
The same seismic sea-wall swell
Of those irrepressible chemicals
Some scientists call love.

The Chemistry Lesson

'Important dates?'
Intones the teacher,
Dodging ricochets
From Waterloo
To World War Two.
Above one boy,
A doodlebug silence;
His mind still trophied
On last night
And her long legs striding
Into his history.

Webbing the world,
Mercator-style,
The class ignores
His reverie: his points
Plotting directions
To her door; his curve
The trembling slope of her left
Shoulder; his world,
The rosebloom latitude,
The linnet longitude
Of her address.

'Forget the eye of the beholder;
Beauty is the ecstasy
Of line.' The teacher illustrates:
Dips his brush in oil,
Strokes the canvas's
Sensuous length.
Words are blurred.
The boy sees only
Her ecstasy of outline
Fusing the palette's
Brilliant lights.

'Remember Euclid,'
The teacher booms.
'Euclid, father
Of circle, triangle,
Rhombus, square.'
The boy feels sorry
For Euclid, recalls
Her geometry,
The construction of her smile;
Conjectures what theorems
She might illustrate.

Languishing in language,
Pestered by the buzz
Of irregular verbs,
The waspish drone
Of conjugations,
Declensions' tedious
Litanies, he thinks
Of her eyebrows' inflections,
Her moods, her voice, how
To translate her signals,
Their future perfect.

'Turn to Hormones.'
He finds the page, notes
'Estrogen', 'testosterone';
Hears words like 'organ',
'Process', 'serving to excite'.
Which the lesson does not.
Oblivious of his own
Cascading chemicals,
He thinks of her, their
Chemistry; would like to know
The formula for love.

'What does he mean,
"I wandered lonely as a cloud"?'
The boy's head is clouded
But not lonely. It has a lake
And trees, and she is there waving,
Dancing, breezing through the daffodils.
In a corner of the field, he plucks
A daisy. 'She loves me.
She loves me not.'
He counts, cheats a little.
'She loves me.'

Students

What I remember most
Of those bedsit days
By the imperturbable Thames
Is waiting for your visit,

Watching you approach,
The sun catching your hair
Like a raven's wing,
And your flowing black dress

Taking focus like a shadow
Finding substance with each
Louder singing step,
And the heavenly ascent

To the tiny attic room
To which your body gave soul
As we unribboned and unwrapped
The gift of each other,

Frantic fingers busy
With the Braille of skin,
And removing our glasses
To study love more closely.

Shadow Love

Strangers meeting
Without greeting
On a sunlit street
Almost passing
Each other by
Despite the mutual
Leap of the heart
Dilation of the eye

They would have
Shyly gone
Their separate ways
Had their shadows
Not paused
Held hands
And taken the riverside walk
Knowing they would follow

Astrakhan

All evening, his leather jacket
Stretched, casual-neat,

Beneath her astrakhan. Silent,
Not dumb, it lay complacent

While he searched for words, cobbling
A vocabulary path to her affections. Leaving,

Helping with her coat was interruption.
The candle almost screamed

Its symbolism. The house red
Blushed. His jacket collar spread

Into a post-enigma smile
As if it had been counting all her freckles.

Werewolf

Cloud peels its blindfold.
A cyclops moon shines

Through the bedroom window, swelling
Tides of teeth and hair and nails.

He lopes across the lawn,
Feet kissing its moist skin,

Ears alert to the silence of birds
And worms burrowing

Shallow catacombs.
Reaching the wood, luminous

Leaves are cats' eyes
And the fox's bark his compass.

He rolls on grass, enjoys
The sensuous fingers of the breeze

Kneading shoulders and back
Then circles trees, picks

Low skies of bluebells
And dances across streams until

Dawn's silver tracers
Force him home. He rests

Beside his sleeping wife; showers
Blue petals on her hair.

Waking, he stands
Before the mirror, pretends

No surprise at skin
Smooth as Jacob's, leans

Into a kiss, wonders
At familiar flowers.

Blue

Blue fades first in a water-
Colour world. A perfect
Picture, she danced through bluebells
In blue dress and ribbon
Under the bluest sky,
And love highlighting
The blue of her eyes.

The insects' camouflage
Has disappeared with flowers
And dress and sky. Only
The bluebottle's buzz remains
And that hair invisibly tied
Since her ribbon bleached
With the blue in her eyes.

Almost a Love Song

Alighting on the alder branch,
The linnet almost lit my afternoon,
Almost pulled the sting from winter,
When something rustled, startled her,
Sent her notched tail jetting through
The electric blue, postponed
The matinee performance of her song.

So like the woman perched
On her chair in the coffee bar,
Freckled fingers tucked like feathers
Underneath her chin,
When something said left nothing
To be said, disturbed the branch,
Cancelled her contralto.

Wishing on a Star

Anointed in dew, rapt
And gift-wrapped in the present of each other,
They relish their perfect moment,
A moment to ribbon
And lock safely away.

Under the night sky's splintered glass,
They wish on a pulsing star,
A star snuffed out
Between finger and thumb
All those light years ago.

Fire etcetera

Lightning gave him the idea.
And the spark of pain
When stone accidentally
Dropped on stone.

Taking a fresh glance
At the world, wondering
How rivers and mountains
Became, he invented god.

Meeting the woman
Was high amp ecstasy
Fusing his brain.
But the wheel?

Would love allow?
Allow? Already the belle dame
Was imagining four.
Under a pram.

Walking the Pram

Against a wash of drizzle,
Sunshine, snow, ascetic
Frost, she made a familiar
Picture walking the pram:

Fleecy blankets cradling her dream,
Feathering her Fabergé nest
As the wheels' hieroglyphics
Scribbled their secret on littered

Streets and laurelled avenues.
Peeping under the hood, she cooed
Her warm wood pigeon vowels,
Rattled the plastic menagerie

On its elastic string, blew
Gentle storms in the windmill
To generate a smile. Everyone else
Were the only ones who couldn't see.

Reef

She struck a reef,
Was shipping water fast,
But despite the splintered wound,
The scissored lightning
Tearing at her sails,
She refused to tilt,
Keel over
Until she felt
The infant
Slide safely down her deck
From bow to stern,
Saw her lowered
Into the tarred
Unsinkable
Lifeboat
Of the midwife's hands.

Fish

She carried from church
Symbols of fish, baptismal tides,
Blood and water trickling
From her Saviour's side,

Unaware of what she carried
In the temple of her body.
Then the shapeless, helpless thing
Caught in the flood of blood,

Dangling at the end of her line,
Flopping on the kitchen floor.
She said it was like a tiny fish,
Lifted it with infinite care.

The high tide mark was red
When she placed it in the basin:
Her little fish that would not leap
The waterfall, could not even swim.

Goosewing

Her goosewing was the best of feather
Dusters, light as air, fluttering

Into crannies inaccessible
As cliffs, its deft flick brightening

The smiles on gilt-framed photographs,
Dispersing thin cloud

From the pride-of-place bottle. Nesting
In the bottle, a clipper whose sails

Would never catch the wind, but understood
The Icarus itch in her shoulders.

The Moses Basket

Because love alone could not promise
A land of milk and honey
To the infant at her breast,

She plied a papyrus basket,
Coated it in bitumen and pitch,
Placed the swaddled baby there

And laid it in the whispering
Reeds along the river's edge,
Watched it drift downstream,

Prayed that it would find some
Pharaoh's daughter. The severed
Umbilical towrope insisted

No return and, no matter
How often she struck the rock,
No waters of forgiveness to soothe

A desert soul. But every day
She climbed the mountain's barren peak,
Looked out for the distant child

Skipping through meadows, through fields
Of fatted cattle; listened
For the industrious hum of bees.

Calling Home

The telephone rings.
Our daughter on the line.
I lift the receiver
From its cradle,
Check that she is fine,
Pass her to her mother
As before. No need to feed,
No nappies to be changed,
But she touches it
Tenderly as skin.
The cord stretches
Umbilically.
She listens, breaks
Into that primal smile,
Translates excited,
Articulate words
Into a gurgle
Or a cry.

At Song, Ambitious Crow

You have exhausted the repertoire
Of 'caw' and 'crah'. I watch you hammer,
Smithy new notes on the August anvil,
Searching, abandoning cliché until
You shape a fresh crow music, beat
Out those brilliant bars adequate
To the joy of bayoneting ants
Trapped in the trenches of the riverbank,
And no cat prowling, no scent of rain,
Only the breeze jetstreaming your wings.

Corncrake

The horsemen of its apocalypse
Dismount to drive a harvester
Round the perimeter of its field.

It tries to hide, protect its young,
Resists breaking cover as, on all
Four sides, phalanx by phalanx

Of grass spears fall. A last-in-the-queue
Creation joke says there were only two
Notes left and one of those was flat.

The craking is his mating call,
Its sharp metallic rasping so like
The reaper whetting his scythe.

Not to Mention

Not to mention granite boulders
Sulking in the grass like gods
Who have lost their worshippers

Or the stonechat in his fifties'
Hairdo grinding out his song
With no chance at the audition

Or the liberal mist
Spraying the hill's armpits
For a heavy date

Or eight geese cranking across the lake
Its water black or silver
At the whim of matador clouds

Or the serried armies of Scots pine
Shoulders straight and looking smart
In uniforms of tailored green

Or the lamb on springs
Sucking up to mother
Its propeller tail all at sea

Or fluorescent come-heathering gorse
Or the willow-warbler's
Antidote to weeping

Or the stream's bent knife
Slicing endless acres
With its copper blade

Or the snowcapped mountains
Up and ready
For the giants' paper chase

To say nothing of the sun
Striding across fields in yellow wellies
Ignoring all those fences and barbed wire

'Bog Standard'

'Bog standard,' intone the press,
Mining their latest truism,
    Digging down
For the deepest seam of insult.

And politicians keep turfing up
The phrase, imagining their tongues
    Slice clean
As slanes through peat and seepage.

Have they not seen corduroy landscapes
Of cutaway bogs, spread lawns of sphagnum moss,
Reels and jigs of rush and meadow thistle,
Sunlight's fingers catching sprays of bogbean,
A spider's stainless steel bridging bog-cotton
And asphodel, the sundew's heliports?

Have they not listened for the plover's golden
Splash or heard formations of Greenland geese
Alight to tug the roots of white breaksedge?
Were they denied the surprise of sand martins
Tunnelling through turf banks, the emperor
Moth basking on heather sprigs, a pipit's

Mottled eggs, nymphs of the emerald damselfly
Below the water's skin? Have they not lingered
Inhaling bog myrtle's perfume or imagining
What torcs, what gold and chalices lie hiding
From the Viking axe? Do they not recognise
The great elk's antlers echoing through mist?

I remember snug turf fires
Curing bacon on chimney hooks,
    Boiling kettles
Cosied in soot, sparking fireflies,

Incense blessing every corner
Of the room, the pelican earth's self-
    Sacrifice consumed
In butterfly flames, setting the standard.

No Fingerprints

Winter sent her warning weeks ago,
Told families to shop, turn up the central
Heating and prepare to hibernate:
Protection of a kind, like painting
Front doors with the blood of a lamb.

Then she donned her camouflage of white
Hands, white cape, white boots,
White skull, and walked invisible
By the glittering, frosted trees.
Now she is well into her mischief:

Her thin crone laughter freezing
Hearts like water in lead pipes.
She sets her skidding traps on every highway,
Leaves sidewalks littered with brittle bones
And, after dark, climbs in the draughty

Windows of the aged poor,
Stabbing with a frenzy of icicles.
Even if she could be found, bound,
Handcuffed and stood before a jury,
Could they reach a 'guilty' verdict in her case?

Icicles leave no fingerprints,
And character witnesses would swear
That she spreads her beauty like a bridal dress,
Lets children glow in immaculate snow
And waves her wand to ice their skating ponds.

Hedge School

Come read the pages of bramble and briar.
Come watch the breeze's fingers flick the score
For blackbirds in smart jackets and pressed tails.
Come smell the incense in dawn's thurible

And listen to the bluebells' gentle chime.
Be starstruck by the lesser celandine's
Low constellation. Admire the blueprint
For the chaffinch's cup-nest, the quaintest

Stories from a redwing's travelogue,
The wren's timid drama. Come see the dog-
Rose petal, brass moth and brimstone butterfly
Illuminate the manuscript. By the light

Of the flickering haws, come sit, come look
Before they make a bonfire of the books.

In the Garden of the Chameleons

A butterfly disappears
Into a rock. Look.
There must be dozens:
That tip of peacock
Feather, that stone
On the gravel path,
Those blown rose petals,
The darker patch of creosote
On the fence, that fist
Of forget-me-nots,
That clever spray,
That glint of quartz,
That chip of bark,
That leaf of copper beech
Beaten on the August
Anvil, that other leaf
Not swaying with the sudden
Breeze, that shimmering
Heat haze. Look.
Look. I don't see
Them either.

Female Nude, circa 1916

North of the Somme, the birds stop
Singing, sensing silence is the anthem
Fit for no-man's-land, for foetal
Bodies drowned in mud, draped
Like weekend washing across lines
Of viper wire. Spent shells

Nest in craters, nothing blue
And speckled waiting for a tapping beak
But everywhere the litter of limbs
And bayonets red with strangers' blood.
In frontline trenches, lovesick
Soldiers pencil notes as time

Ticks towards the whistles
For over-the-top commands, about
The time a police commissioner
On the Rue Taitbout is
Tearing down Modigliani nudes,
Affronted by full frontal pubic hair.

Ringing the Changes

Like metal tulips
The village bells fluttered
In the butterfly breeze,
Chimed their repertoire of praise.

Then war stormed ditch and wall,
Scaled the belltower,
Smelted the iron tongues that called to prayer,
Wounded the innocent air.

Verica's Song

Verica's song has warm hands,
Hands to cup a speckled egg,
Its score a mother's breath
Stooping over cradles.

A chip from the chorus of the Hebrew slaves,
A stranger to Schiller's 'Ode to Joy',
Its skin is chapped
But soft as any lullaby.

It kisses wounds but cannot
Kiss them better,
Breaks the fall
Of the farthing bird.

Flickering in the gloom,
It never cursed the darkness
But tried to counterpoint
The Mengele duet of twins.

The mouth of its river
Speaks of Hokusai's wave,
Of bamboo groves
And meadow butterflies,

June irises, summers
Kindled with azaleas.
Its scale is the rising
Roofs of bright pagodas,

Its dream a picnic in the shade
Of weeping cherry trees,
Shimmering kimonos
In the tea garden's silk breeze.

Its No mask, moulded in compassion,
Sings 'yes' and 'yes' and 'yes';
Its smoke the halo of volcanic
Cloud above Sakura-jima.

Verica's song is Japanese.
Its lyrics best translate
As the tattooed angel wing
That shielded her from Auschwitz.

The Fortune Teller

The fair came to the Fair Green every spring,
Springs that melted like pink candy floss,
That echo with the noise of tents and stalls,
Wheels of fortune, dodgems, carousels,
The shooting galleries and blur of chairoplanes,
Swing boats so high that you could snatch a star.

And every year, predictable and fresh
As daffodils, the fortune teller came.
Whatever her name, it was always
Gypsy Rose Lee: raven hair, a tango
Skirt, bracelets jangling on both wrists,
The half-door to her painted caravan.

Outside, a giggle of girls swapped tales
About the rides, pretended to ignore
Cat-whistles from the boys. Reluctant
To be first to mount the steps, they counted
Copper coins, agreed that sixpence was a small price
For the future, for knowing what was down the line.

Zagreb's Savska Cesta was an Auschwitz
Holding jail with bars that shut out spring.
No fairground music here, no epicure
Stray piebald savouring the grass. But thirteen
Women and a bucket of slops to a cell
With concrete floor, one high window, the stars

Well out of reach. No tents. No caravans
With crystal balls imprisoning the tall
Dark, handsome strangers. Instead, the Japanese
Lady who spread her warm, protective wing
Around the thirteen-year-old child and sang.
She wore no camisole, no turquoise bracelet,

Gypsy dress. Blessed at reading palms,
Unerringly her finger traced the paths
And alleyways of each one's history,
Clicked the combinations to their past.
Here no silver coins betrayed the future
As she declined to mention what was down the line.

Madonna of the Crossfire

Under the Madonna's heel,
The serpent's crushed head.
Stone serpent, stone heel,
Stone Virgin's dress and veil
Torn by shrapnel; nose and mouth
Disfigured, one eye blind,
The debris pocking convent lawns
That spread like Eden before the fall.

Now the Star of Bethlehem
Is a flash of sniper fire;
Angels drop the 'glorias'
From their repertoire;
Shepherds leave their bleating flocks
To the appetite of wolves
And, instead of wise men bearing gifts,
Tanks proffer shells, spit flame.

Under the Madonna's heel,
The serpent's crushed head.
But the outstretched hands
Dispensing peace are shattered
At the wrists, scattered
Where silence amplifies
The ricochet rattle
Of the serpent's tail.

Cinderella

They have lost touch,
The kids who touchingly
Touched while the music
Cannoned 'round the dancehall

Walls. Her midnight
Taxi did not wait;
A soft word saw to that.
And he never found

A foot to fit the shoe
As she lived in a no-go
Zone. He has not danced
Since the incident

With his knee that night,
And she still wakes plucking
From her hair the feathers
That deny her flight.

Migrants

Geese crank north in plump formation,
Conversing in metallic vowels,
Ignoring borders, air corridors.

Swallows target the sun, darting
Due south, stitching aerial tapestries,
Embroidering bright futures.

From Mexico to the Bering Sea,
Whales tumble and churn the brine road.
Not a passport between them.

Salmon know nothing of fences,
Flail and flash up waterfalls,
Pay toll to the brown bear's claw.

Eels daub their faces, wriggle, commando-
Style, across midnight fields
As if attempting the Rio Grande.

And, regular as clockwork, cuckoos
Taxi down with forged papers,
Guarantee summer with their song.

Advising Churchill

My nest was the attic room eyrie,
Hers was the bedsit halfway
Up the carpeted, Georgian stairs.

Exotic as a lorikeet
With her flaming hair and plumage
Of neckscarf and flowing gown,

She would intensely chatter
About how she spent the morning
Advising Winston on the top deck

Of the 24 bus
And the afternoon taking tea
With the Queen at Sandringham.

When they came with municipal nets,
There was just a brief and frantic
Fluttering outside her door,

Scarcely a leaf disturbed
To mark a passing freedom
Churchill might have fought for,

A tale that would have quite
Distressed her majesty at tea.
I hoped her cage would not be small,

That they would keep her outdoors
But away from any draught,
And feed her nectar every day.

For weeks, climbing the stairs,
I watched my step, careful
Not to snap a twig.

Becoming Marie

It started with her hair. They told
Her how it spun the sun, curled
In cataracts about her shoulders.
She made a note about her hair.

They told her that her eyes were deep
Lagoons reflecting the blue shimmer
Of sky, the silver lode of stars.
She made a note about her eyes.

They told her that her mouth was wide
And full, touched by an artist's brush,
That truth was dancing on her lips.
She made a note about her mouth.

They told her that her ears were neat
With perfect lobes, equipped to hear
The lark at praise, the whispering snow.
She made a note about her ears.

They told her that her hands were strong
And delicate, her fingers fit
For harp, piano, the touch of skin.
She made a note about her hands.

They told her that her feet had mountaineers'
Endurance, a ballerina's grace,
Would leave a golddust print on sand.
She made a note about her feet.

They crowded her with places, dates,
The information overload
Of instant heritage. That's how
She knew her name, confirmed her birth.

The walk, the smile, the fingerprints,
The handwriting's bright rills, her voice's
Piccolo trills were also
So becoming for Marie.

'Look, No Words!'

Head over handlebars
Was a lost moment.
Calling, 'Look. No hands,'
Is clear. And picking the gravel
From my knee is painfully clear.
But nothing of the freefall,
The flying into mystery,
That fraction of death.

And another, longer, limbo moment
The day I lost the word-hoard,
Could not name the bluebells,
Grass, the spider clouds,
The quivering arrowhead leaves
On the silver birch,
The sun nesting
On the horizon.

No boasting then.
No pride before the lexical fall
More painful and spectacular
Than head over handlebars.
No words to tag the mute emotion.
And nothing like Adam
Invited by the Lord
To name every fowl and beast.

The Ghost in the Stone

Capsized beside the forget-
Me-nots, the first stone lay
Rough, sharp, whitewashed.

Lifting it revealed a world
Of earwigs, worms, woodlice
In their cool sarcophagus.

And the first cup was chipped china,
Its blue obsequious willows
Dipping in blue streams.

By night, the river fished
The moon's and stars' reflections;
By day it was the glassy stage

Where sunlight laced its dancing
Shoes. The first bell was the angelus
Dispelling morning frost,

The first flower a daisy
Squeezing through cobbles
Like the last of the toothpaste.

Everything bakery fresh,
Steaming in the windows
Of my first dawn. Today's

Cup takes its measure
From blue willows. The river
Sags under history and myth,

Ripples to the sun's encore.
Bells chime the faintest
Echo of belief. The day's

Eye blinks in the shadow
Of graveside immortelles.
Recycled time ticks

Slowly as I finger
The green marble in my pocket,
So much smoother than love.

Exile

A muffled sound like letters on the mat
Was the first sign, and distant dustclouds
Blurring her horizons. One by one,
Buildings collapsed, to reappear

Unnatural as changelings. Unused
To moving with the times, the times moved
All about her. Rubble
Tightened its garrotte around her terraced

Crib. Friends fled their homes:
Aviaries disturbed by storm,
Habitats reoccupied
By birds of different feathers.

She meets them in the high street
And the corner shop: new species,
Young, exotic in their plumage.
Estranged by rhythms of alien song,

She sits alone; dusts the receiver
On the telephone. Through the kitchen window,
She watches sparrows stabbing at her crumbs.
Through the gas bill's window, she warms

To the reassurance of her name. Through the night,
She rests her elbows on the bedroom window,
Recalls the course of a hidden star,
Ponders the metaphysics of bulldozers.

Credo

I believe in the speed of light,
That $E = mc^2$,
That we spin ninety three
Million miles from the sun,
That matter is composed of atoms.
I believe in the big bang theory,
In the mystery of black holes,
The Hubble constant,
In neo-Darwinism and DNA.
I believe that the moon keeps
The same face to the earth,
That the Milky Way spills
Billions of stars.

And I believe such beliefs
Can be painlessly amended
By a bigger telescope,
A 'Horizon' programme,
A chat in the pub.

But the visceral credos
Spooned with love:
That God built the world
In a six-day week,
Adam and Eve, free will,
The fall, redemption,
Heaven waiting
Like a father's hands
To catch the soul?

Bitter the taste
Of mother's milk certainties
Losing orbit,
Turning relatively sour.

Gardener

That '*Noli me tangere*' love
Is fine for heaven,
Not for heaven on earth.

Imagine her surprise
In the Easter garden
Flecked with roseblood petals

When he called her name
And the boulder rolled
From her eyes revealing

Not the gardener
But the man whose feet
Were washed with tears

And towelled with tumbling hair.
Then to hear him say,
'Don't touch!'

So many Marys
Asked to forget when desire
Was water to the rose of love.

Mongoose in Paradise

He was onto a bestseller. Perhaps
The greatest story ever told.
He would start by creating man.
Not generic man, but shape a fistful
Of earth into a hairy, chest-thumping,
Preen-yourself-in-the-mirror
Vine-swinger, breathe into it
A living soul and call him Adam.
Then he would invent emotion,
Make him lonely, a needle
Without a magnetic pole.
Enter Eve, stage left, via
The rib removed from Adam's side
As he slept and dreamed
A young man's urgent dream.
Their bliss would be absolute
In this garden of Paradise.
No toil, no pain, no death.
Just complete happiness so
No need for redemption's epic tale,
No waiting for messiahs,
No star above a crib in Bethlehem
And wise astronomers lugging gifts,
No changing water into wine,
No stinking Lazarus rising from the dead,
No parables competing with the psalms,
No sermon on a mountaintop
Scraping heaven's floor, no Judas kiss,
No Roman soldiers nailing to a cross,
No incandescent resurrection,
No dove dramatic with tongues of fire,
No ... No readership. Any agent
Worth her ten per cent could tell.
So to shake it up, jazz it up, give it

A buzz, he would make one rule
With a fearsome forfeit,
Chalk 'Forbidden Fruit'
On the tree of knowledge
Then introduce the devil of a villain.
Disguised as the slimiest snake,
He would lie through his fangs,
Persuade them to bite the apple
Promising they would be as gods.
Then the figleaf shame,
The hiding in bushes,
The expulsion like kids from boarding school,
The Securicor angel with his flaming sword.
And that would be just chapter one.
Imagine the royalties.
But the best laid plans ...
The serpent twines around the tree,
Remembers to watch his sibilants,
Practises his best lines for doe-eyed Eve.
So easy peasy; a trap effortlessly sprung.
And then the mongoose.
That bloody mongoose.

The Sands of St. Enodoc

Sandlocked, the church surrenders
To Atlantic siege, to the gale's
Huge shovelling sealing up its door,

But temporarily. The steeple's snorkel
Breathes the green sheen of waves,
The gulls' falsetto, ragwort,

Thyme, the shadow of pine,
The bumblebee's flying tiger,
The laughter of children climbing stiles.

And already the parson,
Like a nimble angel,
Is shinning down the rope

From slate roof to the slate floor
Polished by pilgrim feet.
In the damp silence, witnessed

By windows' pale green eyes,
He renews his pact with lamps and pews,
With Norman arch and rounded roof,

The arcade's Bodmin granite, the fluted font.
His prayer before the altar keeps
The building's consecration intact.

Ascending the rope, he sees
The spire's finger point to heaven,
Knows he has kept open the right of way.

Forgery

The night sky was a picture:
A jet-black velvet wash
Highlighting stars
Like a tray of jewels,
And a bullfrog moon
Pulsing with pride.
In the bottom right hand corner
The letters G O D
Which some experts dispute.

Galileo and the Birds

Urban VIII disapproved of the song
Of the birds in the Vatican gardens,
Vernacular lyrics distracting him
From plain chant and canonical
Hours. So he decreed their silence.

He disapproved too of Galileo,
His canticle of the Copernican sun,
And arranged a walk in the garden,
A tour of the holy inquisition's dungeon
And the rack with its knack of stretching the truth.

Recanting in his penitential robes,
A lark sightreading the repertoire of crows,
Galileo knew, as sure as Earth spun
Round the sun, that the birds would return
And sing *fortissimo* their infallible song.

The King's Barber

For the king, the bone comb
Parting hair and the cut
And trim of golden scissors.

For the barber, the cut
Of the royal executioner.
Barber by barber falls

In the gale of his swirling
Sword until mercy
Touches the widow's son.

Spared by silence, his secret
Fevers the tongue. The hell
Of unspoken syllables

Blisters lips, harvests
The mouth's ulcers. Near death,
He curls up in the forest's womb,

Confides in the bark
Of a tree, lopes home unburdened.
Odd that the woodman chooses this willow

To carve the minstrel's harp.
More surprising for the court
When the harpstrings sing.

The storm in the sword subsides.
The king's full goblet ruptures wine
At the shame of horse's ears.

Fresco

On the Sistine ceiling, fingers
Almost touch: Adam's pristine skin

Inching towards the hand of God
Rough from a six day working

Week. Of course they never meet,
Pure spirit and all that, but the metaphor

Succeeds, his grey beard shorthand
For 'eternal', 'wise'. He scans

The lines on Adam's palm. If the Lord
Indeed is a jealous god

What he envies must be touch:
The April rain on Adam's cheek,

A boisterous breeze tousling his hair,
The salt waves' sting over

Sandalled feet, his skin against the skin
Of Eve, tongues too close for language.

The omnipotent finger writes like a pen
Jealous of its word, its own creation.

Adam's Navel

Painting the ceiling was a pain in the neck,
The arm, the lower back. But the headache
Was whether to paint in Adam's navel.

The theology said no: direct creation
By the Uncaused Cause saw clouds of glory
But no need for trailing umbilical cords.

And what next? A scar in his side where the Lord
Plucked a rib to shape the form of Eve?
A patch on the ceiling reserved for the invisible God?

He kept things simple, daubed in the belly button,
Ensured that when the tourists would come and go
They would whisper, not about theology, but of Michelangelo.

'The Praying Hands'

Durer's 'Praying Hands'
Are archetypal,
Touching touchstones
Like Van Gogh's boots and chair.

Shaped, knotted, grained
And veined from labour,
They arch in reverence
Like cathedral oak,

Conjure other hands:
A grandmother's freckled
Knuckles kneading dough,
A mother's fingers

Sculpted by arthritis,
A father's that we know
From photographs,
The warm Braille of a lover's

Skin, infant fingers
Compelling us to count
To ten, a childhood friend's
That hooked us in from drowning.

And history scribbles
On papyrus hands:
A scar from a broken
Jar, liver spots,

Lifelines, veins
Attempting Japanese.
I focus on a thumbnail:
The cap of cloud, the ridges'

Sunset rays, the small arc
Sizzling towards
The cuticle. So many
Hands now sunk in seas

Of separation:
Out of reach, out of touch.
And the sea god deaf
To prayers for their return.

Cezanne's Coins

Perfection is temporary,
Like the fruit in Cezanne's still
Life meticulously poised,
Keeping their geometric pose,
Balancing on coins until

The last brushstroke
When they relax like models
No longer told to hold their smile.
Succulent globes
Tumble, freefall

Into casual orbits
Before the oils on the canvas dry
Fixing that moment
Of apple and peach,
That texture of flesh in its prime.

'The Brontë Sisters'

Stretcher marks witness
The painting's birth,
And the unpainted edge
Lies raw as the roots
Of a Michelangelo,
As Branwell's *pentimento*
Column denying
The triangular composition,
Erasing him from art
As well as life. Temporarily.
The paint reneges, vetoes
Oblivion. Haunting
The canvas, he emerges
In white shirt, black coat
And cravat through the blurred
Sarcophagus pillar.
As ghosts do.

Bresson's Women

The girl's unshuttered eyes
Are wide, alert as a camera;
Her mouth open, lips moist, eager
For kisses and the magic of words.
Cliché breasts pout, full
And smooth as Michelangelo marble.

Behind her, sixty years away,
Another woman thin as shadow.

We guess what sepia images
Developed in the rheum of her eyes,
What histories lie zipped
Behind those rusty lips.
Her breasts hang withered,
Nipples pinned like medals from some war.

The Davidoff

(In Memoriam Jacqueline du Pré)

She died in the wake of the storm.
As hurricane fingers played
Fortissimo across field and garden,
Disease gripped her tight between hungry

Knees, its fierce *arco* sawing
Her strings, releasing her soul
As she released the Davidoff's
Thunder: snapping branches, swirling

Leaves round studio and concert hall
When her bow was a wand placing
The world at her feet, the cello's
Tail-pin earthing her lightning.

Pilgrim's Regress

Arriving at heaven was a downer.
Gates shut, no St. Peter, no recording
Angel inscribing in a golden book,
Not even an echo of cherubim
And seraphim or a T-shirt from their
Last performance. No key under the flower
Pot. Pilgrim read the note again:
'Apologies for inconvenience.
Closure not eternal, just temporary
For essential refurbishment. If you
Would like to wait, directions to limbo
Are under the welcome mat. Even if
You wouldn't, they are there (laugh).
Signed Michael per pro God.
P.S. Do help yourself to coffee
And fresh doughnuts in the lodge.'
He pinched himself, believed the strawberry
Bruise, and the sinking to his knees was not
In prayer. But resilience came riding
On its charger. A muffled expletive,
A quick drag on a cigarette and off
He set, dropping his backpack on the grass,
Needing no Evangelist to point
To wicker gates or distant lights. Knowing
The way, he kicked off his sandals and danced
Through fields of bluebells, deciding joy
Was the compass on which he could rely.
He was too much a gambolling lamb across
The Enchanted Ground to join in sleep the human
Sheep. Sure-footed as a goat, he climbed
The Delectable Mountains, collecting
Purest air and edelweiss. He thought
The ambush of Giant Despair a little
Tedious, explained he was a figment

And watched him disappear. The silver mine
Lining of Lucre Hill held no attraction.
But Vanity Fair was useful; arriving
Late, he warmed his hands by the bonfire.
He hitched a lift on the ring road round
The Valley of the Shadow of Death. Stepping
Down, he spotted the bully Apollyon
Still silly in fish scales and dragon wings.
Pilgrim had outgrown these confrontations,
Just shuffled by, whistling a happy tune,
Watched the fire quench in Apollyon's belly
And the teeth in his lion mouth fall out.
Deciding the Slough of Despond was all
In the mind, he wished its transformation
To a heated pool, dived in for a dozen
Invigorating laps and towelled his tingling
Body in the soothing sun. His last
Steps home kept echoing how his wilderness
World had changed. Lying on the river bank,
He felt his fingers knit with the fingers
Of his very first love outstretched beside him:
Face radiant, body clad in white bikini.
And this time not separated
By the broken glass and razor wire
Of catechism certainties. How would
This new beginning end? Please, Lord, not with
'So I awoke, and behold it was a dream.'

John Clare's Calendar

Predictable, his seasons,
Turning, month by month,
Like a cart's painted wheel
On the old dirt road,
Its orbit even round the axle
Except for occasional bumps and ruts.

Faithful as old sheep dogs,
The months succeed each other:
Winter barking, summer wagging its tail;
Work, customs and games
Beaded like raindrops on a twig,
The thread through letters supporting words.

Not words like 'greenhouse effect'
And 'ozone layer' but '*crowflower*',
'*Higgle*', '*brashy*': a fleecy vocabulary
The collie outflanks and,
At a coded whistle,
Pens in uneven or octet folds.

Crowflower; buttercup
Higgle; work laboriously
Brashy; delicate

Shapings

He shaped words into lead,
Moulded it to bullets,
Tried, unsuccessfully,
To shoot his way out.

He shaped words into hope.
They found him,
Ammunition spent,
Canteen empty on the sand.

He shaped words into prayers.
They rose like helium,
Could not penetrate
The shield of cloud.

He shaped words into water,
Almost drowned in its siren deeps;
Now listens daily for her song
Welcoming him back.

He shaped words into cloth:
An evening dress, a chasuble,
A matador cape.
Such a chameleon.

He shaped words to a harp.
It sang each syllable
Whispered in its ear,
All the secrets of the wood.

He shaped words into wings.
They soared up and away
Before he could
Attach them to his shoulders.

He shaped words to a kiss.
Well, tried
But lacked the other lips
To conspire in its creation.

He shaped words to a stone,
Saw his chiselled name and date of death,
Squatted in its shade to see
Who might bring flowers or pray.

He left the words alone,
Watched them take their clothes off,
Dance naked on the page.
It was all they wanted.

So Like Earth

Each of us a world of our own,
And so like Earth:
A paradise skin
Of rivers, fields and trees;
Playground for fish and tiger,
Symphonies of birds fenced in
By gravity's razor wire.

A paradise
So easily lost,
Vulnerable to December's faulty brakes
Like Earth in the path
Of comet or meteorite

Though more likely
Victim to the enemy within,
The ambush
By cancer, furred arteries,
The clotting brain;
That molten ore from our inner core
To hydrosphere and basalt crust.

And, for the unworldly,
The faint hope of another choir
Beyond the steel-blue wire.

Siren Song

He was hooked on swimming.
Every summer the river called
And he dived in to play.
They quarrelled only once,
That afternoon when sunlight flung
Its net from bank to bank
And his deep, cold friend
Got rough, slapped him
With its current, pulled
Him down five times not three.
Distinctly, he heard bells
But gentle like the twittering
Of birds. And his legs were heavier
Than sinkers on a line.
Then the water lost interest;
No competition there.
Or perhaps he was small fry,
A worthless sacrifice,
And Hickey hauling him by the hair
Was the goddess throwing him back.
Now, sometimes, when the music stops,
He hears only her siren song
And looks down at the water,
A safety net of sorts.

The Dustman Cometh

He lugs those sleek, black, plastic bags
Like the body bags in 'Nam,
But the dustman does not drive a hearse
To collect the relics of our week
And never shouts, 'Bring out your dead'
Although those seven days destroy
The fresh and new, reverse creation.

A tiny slice of history dies here:
The votive daily bread gone stale,
The popped birthday balloons,
The blazing headlines that soon cooled,
The torn page of sheet music,
The hallway bulb that flickered its faint
Star, the holiday's chipped mug.

Week by week, the bags are filled, collected,
Until the sudden week when our turn comes
To be lugged away, liturgically
Lowered into consecrated holes.
And maybe excavated at some distant date,
Unwrapped and dusted down by scholars
Fluent in the language of rags and bones.

Deathwatch

The deathwatch beetle watches out for death.
Extinction's sentinel, something in his
Water warns of endgames, last sunsets,
Of final curtains hearing no applause.
He reruns in his mind the old debate
On dinosaurs. What mystery erased
Those lords of earth? A lethal fist of ice
Or some firework display of meteorite?

He wonders too what googly bowled mankind
A mere three million years ago: *homo*
So *sapiens* bemused by wrist and spin,
Speed of delivery or leg before
What wicket? Or was it simply acid rain
That stopped his play? One thing for sure:
Eventually, they had swapped their whites
For that eternal, problematic night.

Long gone their littered legacies, the clues
To acts of war and theories of love:
The rusty tanks and missile heads, the nuclear
Buttons pulsing on oak desks, the Louvre,
The pyramids, the Taj Mahal, God's finger
Touching Adam's on the Sistine roof,
All swallowed up by earthquake, tide and sand;
No echo of Mozart, Beethoven's Ninth.

Gone too their libraries, their dusty tomes
Thorned with the terror of death's sting; a few
Illuminated with the flickering dream
Of living on in living memory.
The beetle's mutant brain recalls that slim
Hope fusing with the last demise, and sees
Too late a metal snout and tongue of fibre
Glass. Their turn next to inherit the earth.

A Quiet Apocalypse

Those skeletal horsemen thundered
Across the illustrated bible's plains,
Slicing air with scythe and sword.

Perhaps they still storm over battlefields,
Spark cobbled skulls to signal
Fire and flood, famine's filed teeth.

But mostly there's the silence of the worm,
Disease's unreported bloodless coup,
The donkeys of the apocalypse limping home.

Camping Out

The stars' candelabra
Flickered between leaves.
They unzipped the sleeping bag
And held hands walking

Through the wood: silent
Except for the owlhoot,
The fox's red bark.
They found the oak

With their carved initials
And arrowed heart,
Sang as they plucked moonbeams
Like the strings of a guitar.

Then the leisured walk back,
The slipping into their plot's
Green bag, the glance
At their chiselled names

And date of drowning.
They blew out the stars.
The lark intoning lauds
Was their lullaby.

The Dead Room

This is where those final years unspooled,
This musty room embarrassed by cheap curtains
And furnishings he thought of as antiques.

The books range from his Latin prize to paper-
Backs of twenty years ago. His records,
Like good wine, were best when shared. This scratch

Dates from the night they had too little space
To dance, that warp from copper summers
When the doorbell didn't ring, about the time

The postman ceased to call with perfumed letters,
The time windows and door shut tight against
More than the cold. Unfiltered nicotine

Stained ceilings. Sandpainting carpet choked
On histories of dust. Next week, the decorators
Will be in to flay the walls of their

Old skin, remove all trace of DNA,
The frayed specifications of his soul.
And he'll return, a hunkering, locked-out child

Whose parents are not home and have not left
The key. The new tenant will wake at midnight
Startled by the crying at the door.

Watchmaker

Perched like owls, every room was crammed
With clocks; watches were the sparrows.
He picked them up from stalls, junk shops
And car-boot sales, took them in,

Nursed them like birds with broken wings,
Displayed them in glass cases,
Wound them up, reminded them
To sing. His ticking resurrections.

When his own ticking stuttered, grew
Irregular and stopped, the pendulums
Hung limp, the chimes were mute,
Convulsive seconds twitched and died.

We opened up the staking set,
Held him steady on the stand,
Strapped on the eye-loop for a closer
Look. But oil could not revive;

Tweezers and screwdrivers were wands
Without a magic for worn parts.
His nest of jewels lay lustreless.
No donor could replace his spring.

Pick-and-Mix

They said her going was sudden
As if, on impulse,
Pulling on her coat
That last Lancashire Saturday,
She hopped onto a double-decker bus
And bought her ticket. One way.

Dropped off at the gate,
Did she get to choose
('In my father's house
There are many mansions')
Like dipping her hand in a paper bag
To fish her favourite sweet?

And did she choose
A summer weekend in Blackpool
Where dancehalls were the polished floors of heaven
And, buoyed on the Big Band sound,
She swished and glided
Under the low moon's glitterball

Or some Sunday afternoon when you were five,
She in her blue cotton dress
Watching a Carole Lombard matinee
Or singing *sotto voce* in your ear,
You nesting on her dancer's knee
Dipping your fingers in Woolworth's pick-and-mix?

Child Alarm

You came home early in that wooden box.
A sudden ending to your holiday.
Sudden as the out-of-nowhere car
That flashed like some conductor's baton

Knocking your song right out of key
And opening doors I cannot enter. I was not there,
But for mothers the impossible is no excuse.
My arms ache now with the weight of emptiness,

Clutch at memories. Religion's good news
Is lost in the post. Philosophy brings
Only the idea of consolation. But I keep
The child alarm switched on and listen

As you lie cradled in eternity,
Reassured you are not crying in your sleep.

Comfort Blankets

Like a flame-tongued, sword-fingered monster
Guarding the entrance to its cave,
He hugged the comfort blanket to himself,
Gripped it tight in tiny fists. No sharing here.
That privilege reserved for Gran.
He'd take a well-chewed corner from his mouth
And proffer it as if sharing the grail.

When time swooped down on monster wings,
She lay there restless on her island bed.
Our turn to sit like sentinels and watch,
To spoon her water, soften pillows, count
The exhalations of her breath. His turn
To take the blanket in strong hands,
To tuck her gently in against the cold.

Bequeathing Damocles

Each clause clips like scissors,
Snips the long life's impedimenta.
The house, of course, goes to the son.
Rather, the son to the house.
The villa, a home from home
For the favourite daughter.

No gavel here. Otherwise,
An auction house gravity.
In turn, the Steinway,
The silver, the first editions
Claim new custodians.

No surprise
Except for the late Hockney,
Its California light
To dazzle an address
In Bognor Regis.

And no mention of the maverick gene,
Its bright blade glittering
From the ceiling.

Sutures

All we wanted was the lightning.
But the priests rushed in with sandbag
Liturgies, plain-chanting about eternal
Rest, pleading with angels to lead
Him into paradise, sealing our
Seismic loss and bandaging
In palls of ritual.

And Mercury almost as bad,
His anxious sandals fluttering
Like moths, pitying our faultlines,
Anointing wounds of absence
With perfumed promises of the gods.
An over-conscientious guide
Through infernal regions

When all we wanted was the lightning's
Needle, the comfort of stitches
Like a mother mending shirts,
Fingers tying the definitive knot,
Strong teeth snapping thread.
A gift of unhurried healing
For sutured hearts.

Isobel and the Balance of Nature

Next door's toddler
Restores, her bright hair
Lighting up the cave
To which the world retreated
That mourning morning
My mother died.

The redress of one flower
Withering on her bed
As Isobel's petals
Opened to first light
Proffers, like Boethius,
The consolation of philosophy.

Her little light shines
Waving from door and car window,
Surmounting the drive's
Himalayan steps,
Exploring the Vesuvius
Hole in the road,

Gripping her parents'
And Phoebe's hands
On expeditions to the shop,
Wobbling on her plastic
Trike, restoring
The balance of nature.

Some Falling Leaves

Like feathers in a childhood pillow fight,
Leaves fell gently down from the chestnut tree
Outside our door; a tree now felled,
Its roots pulled without anaesthetic,
Cemented to a parking spot, chipped concrete
Reading like some ancient runes.

Across the road, ivy leaves climbed
The hospital wall, gripping toes
And fingers in the mortar between stones.
We plucked them on the way to school,
Placed them between the pages of a book,
Watched them change colour, emaciate to veins.

Soon the hand-in-hand, riverside walks,
Admiring that third thing: bulrushes,
Moon, a floating stick, the willow's
Green umbrella. And too soon the lesson
That the wettest place after a shower
Is under the sheltering leaves.

Then the painted pipal leaves.
One, a tiger sipping its reflection
From the Ganges. Another
Of a Hindu girl, the *bindi*
On her forehead like a tiny sun,
Fingers slender as El Greco's saint.

Now your unseasonal falling,
A silver arrowhead shaken
From its birch, floating soft
As eider, nesting in the clay's
Cool cradle. I press your memory
Between the pages of a favourite book.

Pyramid

The curtain falls on the Royal George Hotel,
Final as the granite doors shuddering down
To seal the burial chamber of some pharaoh.

This is where their curtain opened when
Spotlights caught their drama, fixed them centre stage
Improvising those first faltering lines.

This is where he sent the cards stamped 'Cairo':
Camels, dusty streets, white dishdashas,
Baked walls, a sepia pyramid.

This was the address for urgent love
Notes from the front. Later, the dictated
Letters, photos of the fresh war grave.

Now the theatre is dark, all seven floors
And basement. Plywood blinds the windows, guards
The doors like sentinels with flaming swords.

I hoard the letters like a treasured
Folio. His promises in pencil
And blue ink lie boxed beside the sun-bleached cards.

And the hotel where they fetched and carried,
As if dancing attendance on a king,
Has changed its lease, become their pyramid.

Its four sides face the four points of the compass;
Reed mats decorate the limestone walls;
Chiselled hieroglyphs decode the past.

By day, the lovers wait for gaps in cloud,
Shinny the sun's rays, enter stage left
The open-air theatre of the gods.

By night, they stroll with Isis down cool corridors.
The building's apex takes its bearings, points
To their propitious circumpolar star.